I0108427

It's Reachable

A Short Guide to Your Next Chapter in Life

Maggie Kelly Fenn

Dedicated to Dennis Fenn, my husband of 42 years who supports and loves me unconditionally

Photographs contributed by Brain Narajowski

"My passion is to ..." and many of us end there, verbalizing our dream but never acting on it. Why? Don't go through life not realizing your potential. Necessity, or an "aha" moment can present itself when it's time to create your next chapter. Pam from Chicago pursued a Master's degree in Psychology in her 50's stating, "My children were all leaving and I needed to turn my attention outward. I decided to pursue my dream of becoming a counselor. I once was told we all have just so many pages in the book of life so I didn't want to leave any blank ones." Where are you in your life's journey? Is it time to fill in the blanks? I've learned so much along my life path, sometimes luck, sometimes connections comes into play, but ultimately it is a belief in yourself and working through a process to make it happen.

When you allow yourself to dream, what do you envision for yourself? What would you really like to be doing? Sitting on the train or bus, idling in traffic, where do you wish you were heading instead of your present job? Obstacles can be overcome, false perceptions eliminated, dreams can become a reality.

Now I know we have to be realistic. Many times, I come back from a jog singing along with Celine on my I-Pod until my husband screams, "Please Stop! "At least he does say please. I wish I could sound like her but I was never blessed with the pipes. Be truthful, how many of us sing in the shower envisioning the audience begging for more. I think the true realization for me that I wasn't going to be dissuaded in my aspirations was at St. Luke's Grammar School in Whitestone, New York. I was part of the school choir; the nun in charge tapped me on the shoulder during a rehearsal and asked that I just mouth the song. In other words, lip-synch before Milli Vanilli made it popular. I was smart enough to realize she was really pleading, "Please quit." Sorry, it was wasted effort on her part, I stuck it out but alas no solos. At least, I did get to be part of something I really loved despite my limited capabilities. Lesson learned, we can't all be rock stars, phenomenal athletes, CEO's but we can soar to heights we never believed possible. What follows is a short guide to realize your next chapter. I believe in you, I know you can do it. For starters, I'll fill you in on my journey so far. Did you notice I said, "So Far?"

Chapter One

The first time I vividly remember mapping out my future was the day of President Kennedy's funeral, Monday, November 25, 1963. We had off from school and I was watching with my family the sad events of the day.

I looked out my front window on 22nd Ave; there was that guy I recently noticed locked arm in arm with the new girl from across the street. The previous summer, my friend, Steve (or Fitz as we affectionately called him) walked by with this new kid. He was short, wiry, and I couldn't keep my eyes off him. "Hey Fitz, who's that new friend you were heading to the park with"? I was trying to sound nonchalant. It was Dennis; he lived four blocks away in the Cops and Fireman's Development. That was the area where a lot of New York's Finest settled in the early 50's. My dad was in the NYPD and knew many of the families. I continued to eye him whenever I could and then that fateful day I had the instant realization that he didn't belong with her but with me. At the age of 14, I realized I was going to marry him one day. Sounds crazy, I know, but 42 years later and counting, I guess I knew my heart at a very young age. Don't get the wrong impression though; this innocent catholic schoolgirl didn't make her move until the "other" girl moved away.

My new boyfriend actually confessed that he remembers the first time he set eyes on me. He lobbed the paper each day onto our front stoop or as close as possible. One Friday he came to collect and I answered the door, 12 years old, baton in hand. He said he remembered the skimpy (we didn't say sexy in those days) twirling outfit I was wearing. I remember it well, Kelly green, many sequins, up to my neck but did show some leg. I guess that was the skimpy part. He has made me laugh all these years and I can't imagine my life without him.

Two daughters, two sons-in-law and two grandsons later, we're still laughing and loving but I hardly recognize that 20 year old girl who happily walked down the aisle on Aug. 30th, 1969. Luckily, my husband, now knowing me well, frequently asks along our journey "So, fill me in, what's your next chapter?"

At 20, all I dreamed about was getting married and becoming a mom, having a successful career was a distant third. I looked on with some bewilderment at my 60's era peers "tripping" at Woodstock weeks before my wedding. I wasn't quite a June Cleaver (couldn't afford the pearls) however, I wasn't too attuned yet to burning my bra and having it all as Betty Freidan and Cosmo Magazine were espousing.

We spent the first 5 years of our married life trying desperately to become parents. My husband and I went through lots of tests and procedures, when the nurse handed my husband a Playboy Magazine for one of them, our Catholic school naiveté went out the window. Finally, our great doctor figured out I had blocked fallopian tubes, one simple procedure and voila, nine months later our first daughter was born followed two years later with our second. I was right motherhood was for me. We watched this new show Sesame Street (loved Oscar the Grouch), Electric Company (Morgan Freeman, who knew), played Candy Land, roller-skated, I loved it all. We weren't rich by any means but mom staying at home with the girls was definitely our choice at the time.

Rather quickly, it seemed, our daughters were off to school and spending more time with their playmates. I was joyous they had friends and a life but hey, what about good old mom. Remember me, your chauffeur, cook, cleaning woman, and confidant? That's when I had my first true "aha moment", "WHAT AM I GOING TO DO WITH THE REST OF MY LIFE?"

I had gone to the Mandel School in Manhattan before we were married and became a licensed lab technician in hematology. During my years at home with the girls however, technology had improved tremendously and I knew I'd need a refresher course. Is this what I still wanted to do?

I thought long and hard about my strengths and weaknesses in planning my next step. I was always a life-long reader and loved history so I decided teaching was for me. It also had the added benefit of similar vacation schedules with the girls so day care wasn't an issue. I went to the local State University of New York campus, talked to an advisor and decided I could manage going back to school for a degree in education. My husband was supportive as always and said we'll figure out a way to afford it. Another very vivid memory, I'm driving home from the initial interview, pounding on the steering wheel screaming, "I can do this", "I know I can do this," "I can earn a college degree; I'm only still in my 30's."

I loved the learning process despite the fact that the majority of my fellow students were born around the time I was married. I soon understood the true meaning of "Generation Gap". Guns & Roses instead of the Beach Boys, who's this Def Leppard, what happened to Petula Clark? I could still live out my singing fantasy however, Pat Benatar and I frequently belted out, "Hit Me with Your Best Shot" on my way to school.

Graduation day, now 40 but ready to take on the world, I had to drag our teenage girls out of bed to attend the ceremony with my husband. Typical for that age, they weren't all that impressed that their mom was getting a college degree however, I was elated.

The school that my youngest daughter attended was actively searching for a teacher. Despite her abject fear that I would totally embarrass her by doing something lame, I took the job. Luckily, she'd graduated by the time I did do something lame. I planned a lesson to commemorate the 50th anniversary of D-Day. My father-in-law had been a WW II bomber pilot and had written an emotional and faith filled diary when he went out on each of his missions.

I read an excerpt to the class and then showed parts of the movie, Memphis Belle. That plane, a B-17, was an exact replica of the one Walter Fenn piloted. Unfortunately, I hadn't fully reviewed the actual clip and it included very colorful language. Children being children couldn't wait to get home to tell their parents what Mrs. Fenn let them see and hear.

It caused a minor skirmish at St. John's Parochial School. Luckily, I was generally well liked and my profuse apologies with a promise to be more diligent in the future sufficed. I did mention my daughter had graduated by then, right?

Chapter 2

"Mag, Do You Want to Move to Chicago?"

My husband came home from work one day posing that question. He had a great job opportunity in the Windy City. I didn't hesitate for a moment, "Sure, why not." Our girls were away at college; the house now seemed too big. "I'm ready for our next adventure, let's try something new." I had to give up my teaching job, which was the hardest part, but I was confident something else would come along.

The moving man walked into our new apartment in Chicago and shouted, "Wow, did you guys change your lifestyle." He had gathered all our possessions out of rural Goshen, New York where we were surrounded by farms and transferred them to a 40th floor high-rise. My husband and I had decided to become city dwellers. We both realized at that stage in our life, it was perfect. No leaves to rake, no snow to shovel, and in the city since we walked everywhere, great exercise. OK, so now I had a great metropolitan location, full of opportunities, what do I do?

I substitute taught for a while, however, a full time position wasn't presenting itself. My husband continued to be busy at work, enjoying new challenges and travelling a few days every week. I realized I was creeping towards 50. How do I remarket myself?

My computer skills at that time were rudimentary so I enrolled at a local city college to upgrade my proficiency. I wasn't sure what else I was qualified for so I enlisted the help of an employment agency. I was soon hired as a receptionist at a large architectural/engineering firm. I quickly discovered what some consider a menial job to be very challenging and an excellent way to hone my interpersonal skills.

I also enjoyed the diversity of working and interacting with adults instead of children and adolescents. The company was a mini United Nations. Quite a few employees were from divergent backgrounds and I enjoyed hearing about their journeys to America, their specific duties at work and their trials and tribulations. Yes, working at a front desk is really bartending without the drinks, a perfect spot to stop and share your woes. I loved it! Feeling more confident in an office environment and wanting additional responsibilities, I moved on to a different firm and became the office manager; the personal interactions were always the favorite part of my days.

Chapter 3

There are Always More
Mountains to Climb

My husband had always used me as a sounding board for all his work related decisions. I knew he really valued my opinion and advice. Coupling that with my new corporate experience, I started exploring some local schools about obtaining a Master's Degree in Psychology. At first, self-doubt crept in, "Am I crazy?" I was in my mid 50's, we had to get serious about planning for retirement, and how could we afford more education?

Again, I vividly remember being on the city bus en route to work envisioning myself counseling people in distress. We now had a financial advisor and he figured out a way to make it affordable. So, 15 years later and surrounded again by students half my age, I was back at school. More generation gap moments but this time, I latched onto a fellow "older" student and we blended in just fine. Timing again, I knew I was where I was supposed to be in my life's journey. Psychology is fascinating and to learn from professors and doctors with years of experience was exhilarating. My practicum year was daunting, humbling and immensely gratifying, to be in a position to help others in distress, another gift.

Anticipating graduation, I sent out lots of resumes and tried networking but rejections came my way. This time my age did hinder me; all of my interviewers were years younger. A young lady at a local women's clinic said I wouldn't be a good fit, "You don't seem to have a feminist zeal", Ouch! I thought about continuing for a PhD, it would create other opportunities but more schooling in my late 50's and more expense? I decided it wasn't the right time. Our oldest daughter was about to make us grandparents for the first time and I offered to babysit our new grandson part-time. Of course, she jumped at the suggestion. I couldn't miss the opportunity; Brady and I have spent many special moments together.

Chapter 4

"Mag, How about a Move to California"

When your husband asks that question on a day that's 17 degrees below, it's a real easy answer. It was an opportunity for him to oversee a new California office while also phasing into retirement. We've now decided we love it so much; it's becoming our permanent home. We've become active in the local chapter of the Red Cross and meeting incredibly dedicated volunteers.

My last chapter, I doubt it, I'm planning to be active for many more years to come. How many careers is that so far, I'm now 62 and I've been a hospital lab technician (20's), teacher (40's), receptionist & office manager, (40's & 50's) counselor, grandma and Red Cross volunteer (50's & 60's).

I want to help you create your next chapter by using the methods I've employed along my journey.

Believe it can happen, start a next chapter journal and begin working on the steps!

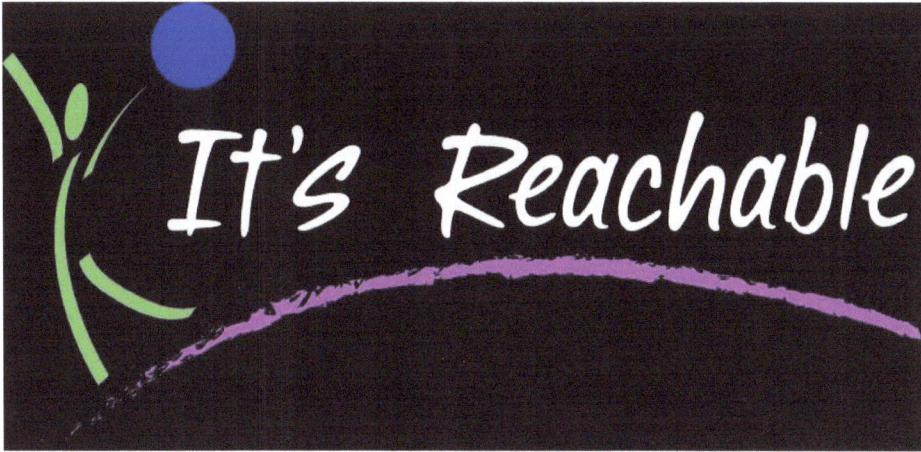

The It's Reachable method is a five step approach to realizing your next chapter.

R= Research

E=Eliminate Obstacles

A=Act "As If"

C=Create

H=Happiness, Get high on your accomplishment

Research

Use the Inter-Net; it's like Child's Play

Thoroughly investigate, inquire, discover, scrutinize, and examine. Do you get the picture? We often have pre-conceived notions about professions we aspire to. The first step in achieving your next chapter should be an exhaustive inquiry on all aspects of your next career. I previously worked with a young architect who loved to bake. She enrolled in an evening culinary class and discovered her true passion. She now uses her creativity in creating pastries instead of buildings. Get that journal out and start taking notes.

Instant information is at your fingertips; you'll find a limitless amount of information. Interested in sports management? Google gives over 28 million hits.

Find as many people as you can who are already in the profession you desire and exhaustively pick their brain about pros and cons. Find an apprenticeship that could fit into your schedule. If you're thinking of a business such as retail, work part-time, watch, listen and learn.

Take a class at a near-by university, community college, or city center. People in a myriad of professions give classes in their communities usually at a very nominal fee.

The Bureau of Labor Statistics, http://www.bls.gov/ offers two great publications to help guide you in your new endeavor. *The Occupational Outlook Handbook* is revised every 2 years and gives information on training, education needed, earning potential, and working conditions. *The Career Guide to Industries* provides links to information about specific job markets in your state.

CareerOneStop, http://www.acinet.org/ is an exhaustive compilation of career information including job search sites. You can click on your state, select your education level, and find job info and opportunities. Learn about future employment trends, the field of Home Health Care Aides is expected to increase by 46% in next 10 years. The Baby Boomer generation is getting older and we'll want assistance!

A four-year degree doesn't necessarily guarantee life-long employment. Mid-skill occupations, defined as needing more than a high school education but less than a four-year degree, are rising in demand and can be obtained through associate's degrees or certificate programs. Some examples are dental hygienists, diagnostic medical sonographers, and legal assistants. An Oct. 2009 edition of the Milwaukee Journal predicted a 46% increase in mid-level job opportunities between the years 2006-2016.

Here is where research is important, however. During tough economic times, it's easy to be lured into trade schools that seemingly offer guaranteed lucrative job opportunities. Unfortunately, these claims are often times misrepresented while the student is incurring additional student loans. The New York Times highlighted these exaggerated promises in a March 2010 article and again in March 2011; some for-profit institutions have a thousand recruiters and only one employee charged with job placement. Bottom-line, if a school is sounding too good to be true, has heavy-handed recruiting practices and offers seemingly limitless financial aid, BEWARE! The Better Business Bureau website http://www.bbb.com allows consumers to check out a potential school and its rating, reliability reports and history of complaints. It also offers tips on how to avoid on-line "diploma mills".

Do you Twitter, use You Tube or MySpace? We all know by now the story of Mark Zuckerburg creating Facebook in his college dorm room. He's just one of many individuals who have used their internet savvy skills to create sites now used by millions. Two new hot careers for technophiles are Social Media Experts and Information Systems Security Professionals.

An Education Today section in a January 2010 edition of The Chicago Tribune reported that companies are hiring "social" managers to monitor many on-line sites to improve their product service capabilities. The Bureau of Labor Statistics recently predicted a significant increase in the need for experts in information security. The University of Denver and Villanova University are two institutions that offer on-line Master's certificates in this expertise.

I sincerely hope by this time, you're starting to feel like there are NO EXCUSES-IT'S REACHABLE. Get started, absorb all information and take the time to investigate, envision, and most of all BELIEVE.

Eliminate Obstacles

"It is very rare that you meet with obstacles in this world that the humblest man has not faculties to surmount."

Henry David Thoreau

Here is where TRUE COMMITMENT is NEEDED!
Webster's Dictionary defines commitment as, "the act of binding yourself intellectually or emotionally to a course of action". "I just don't have the knowledge, the time, the money; people have told me I'm crazy, I'm not confident enough!" ALL EXCUSES!

External Barriers:

Knowledge-Step one Research should be giving you the tools to start obtaining the expertise you need. If you still don't feel ready, take more time learning and researching. There does come a moment, however when enough research has been done and it's time to REACH!

Time-it doesn't have to happen tomorrow. If it's something you really want, you take the time. You reprioritize and plan your day making chapters evolve; even a half hour a day can make a difference. Discuss your desire with spouse and family; work out your alone time. Rely on them to help you carve out the time. Find a friend who wants to create their next chapter, become each other's enabler, and time-share.

Money- finances is a hurdle that oftentimes seems insurmountable. You can explore many avenues for monetary assistance. The largest source of free money is through federal and state grants.

Investigate http://www.collegescholarships.org for extensive information concerning grants plus available scholarships and student loans. Monetary assistance doesn't just exist for high school seniors; there are many programs that are specifically designed for non-traditional students. Your local and state government also has grant monies available. Individual universities offer specific grant money for certain fields of endeavor; check them out in your area.

Want to pursue culinary school? The Culinary Trust offers grants. How about insurance? State Farm offers assistance. One of my personal favorites is Raise the Nation, a non-profit corporation assisting single mothers wanting to continue their education or need help paying student loans.

http://www.educationconnection.com also gives information on grants, scholarships, and loans. Also, check out eligibility requirements for tax credits.

Is your next chapter opening up a small business? Go to http://.ww.sba.gov for help, guidance, and info on monetary assistance, licensing, and permits.

Feeling entrepreneurial? Job lay-offs have given many an impetus to start up a small business. Accion USA is a nonprofit microfinance organization that gives an average loan of $7000 and has already helped more than 13,000 people in the US.

http://www.score.org helps small businesses, offering free advice on starting-up, buying franchises, improving sales, placing your business on the web, etc.

Go to your own bank, sit down with an advisor, discuss your personal finances, and let them help you map out a plan.

Internal Obstacles:

"I know I really can't do this", "So many people have told me I'm crazy". There's nothing more satisfying than defeating the odds and more often our own psyches are our inhibiters. It can come from friends, family members, and acquaintances who think they're giving well- meaning advice but actually are squashing our dreams thinking it's unreachable. Our own upbringing might have instilled feelings of inadequacy or a sense of just being content with what you have. Counseling is available whether it's life coaching, mental health, or someone you know who has your best interests at heart, a true CHEERLEADER!

Your parish, church, synagogue, or community center offers counseling services, many offering sliding scale fees to make it affordable. Take advantage of this if needed to bolster your confidence and self-esteem!

Get out that journal again, write down the obstacles you had initially perceived and create an action plan for eliminating/minimizing each one. Plan a foreseeable target date to achieve it. Keep going back and check them off as they are eliminated.

Act "As If"

"Live as if you were to die tomorrow. Learn as if you were to live forever."

Mahatma Gandhi

The concept of acting "As if" has its root in the teachings of the German philosopher, Hans Vaihinger. We are capable of creating a world for ourselves that supports our true vision. You've done the research; you're working on overcoming your obstacles, now start acting as if your next chapter is within sight. Take the first bold step and talk about it to spouse, friends, and family. Publicly stating it makes it more real, actually hearing the words coming from your own mouth makes it reachable. Start envisioning yourself in that new role or environment. Whether travelling to work, taking a ten-minute break or before you drift off to sleep, make mental images of yourself immersed in your new career. I had the idea for this book for months and had actually started writing and planning it before I gathered up the confidence to tell my husband, my lifelong confidant. After that first burst of courage, telling our daughters, family members and new acquaintances came easier.

I mentioned earlier my love of reading; I especially love biographies. A few years back I picked up, *The Invisible Wall* by Harry Bernstein. Harry started the book at the age of 93 after losing his wife of 67 years. He's now writing his third book.

Ben Cathers started his first business venture, a web marketing, and advertising site geared towards teens at the tender age of 12. He went on to hosting a radio show at 17 and today runs social media initiatives for Lightspeed Financial. These are just a few examples of individuals, young and not so young, who believed in their capabilities and acted on it.

So start telling the world, "I'm onto my next chapter and this is what it is".

Research √

Eliminate Obstacles √

Act "As If" √

Now Create

"Life isn't about finding yourself. Life is about creating yourself."

George Bernard Shaw

Now is the time to create what you've been working towards. This could actually be the easiest step. You've been acting, "as if" and now dive in. Why do I use this metaphor? A few years back I wanted to do a triathlon with my husband. He was a lifelong swimmer; I however always looked like Fido doing the dog paddle. Our local health club recommended a swim coach; at 5:30 am before work I would meet him at the pool to try and look like Michael Phelps. The day of the race, excited and nervous, I jumped into the lake and immediately started to hyperventilate. My husband was in the heat ahead of me so I didn't have him to calm me. I was totally panicking and holding onto a rope at water's edge. A spectator saw me, and screamed into my face, "You can do this! "Instead of sobbing, I took a moment and thought about how hard I'd worked to learn how to swim. I slowly regained my confidence and away I went, I finished! A total stranger had made the difference. This is why I believe in you; amazing things are possible if you put in the work, time, effort and most of all have the belief in yourself.

Create is really an ongoing two-step process. First, open up your store, start your home business, begin your new position. Take all the ingredients you've accumulated and bake that cake.

Now when you start baking, here comes the second part. You realize as you go along, if I add this second ingredient, I know I can enhance the flavor. When I started my second office position as an administrative assistant/office manager, I quickly realized there wasn't enough to keep me busy. There's nothing worse than sitting watching the clock tick instead of realizing, "Wow, it's time to go home." I had to be inventive in creating additional responsibilities and getting my boss to champion it.

Once you're enmeshed in your dream, keep inventing ways of enhancing and improving. Your journey is never over; you've worked so hard to get to this point. Constantly think outside the box and use all those ideas you've accumulated ever since you starting envisioning your next chapter.

Happiness - Make it Endless

"To despise riches, may, indeed be philosophic, but to dispense them worthily, must surely be more beneficial to mankind."

When I read this quote by an unknown author, Bill Gates came to mind. He decided to retire from his life-long passion and with his wife, Melinda, create a worldwide philanthropic foundation. Riches don't have to be monetary however; it comes from work that provides personal fulfillment, provides for the well-being of our family, and in some manner helps others.

This last step, get high on your accomplishments should be a lifelong goal. The Zen Buddhist leader, Thich Nhat Hanh has said, "We can make the happiness of many people even if we don't have a penny in our pocket." My husband and I met a young couple years ago in Argentina. We lived in Buenos Aires for a work related project. This couple befriended us knowing we only knew rudimentary Spanish and were quite unfamiliar with the city. It was evident they were living on a limited income. The husband and wife placed a mattress on the floor to sleep at night and gave their three children the lone bed in their one room apartment. They invited us over for delicious dinners and brought presents up to our two girls on Christmas. They had few possessions yet were full of kindness and obviously a happy and content couple. A prime example of Hahn's quote, it can take very little. Always take the time to enjoy what you have achieved in life, big or small.

I'm fascinated by the resilient nature of individuals; two people facing similar obstacles can create very dissimilar lives. Researchers are concluding that individuals have an innate capacity for resiliency. Studies also indicate that the support of just one individual, oftentimes through a simple word, can make all the difference. Throughout this book I've been saying, "I believe in you" and I do. I believe in the universal human spirit and what it's capable of achieving.

"Don't judge those who try and fail, judge those who fail to try."
Unknown

"Success isn't merely an accumulation of material goods. It may not even be being CEO of a prestigious worldwide company. Success should be redefined as the process in getting there, how one gets there, and earning the right to be there. Success cannot be considered success if one attains the top of his or her field at the expense of others, ethically, morally, or legally."
Conversations with Teen Entrepreneurs

"Excuses abound, it allows stagnation. Fulfillment comes from action, believe in you, enjoy the journey, START NOW!"

Maggie Kelly Fenn

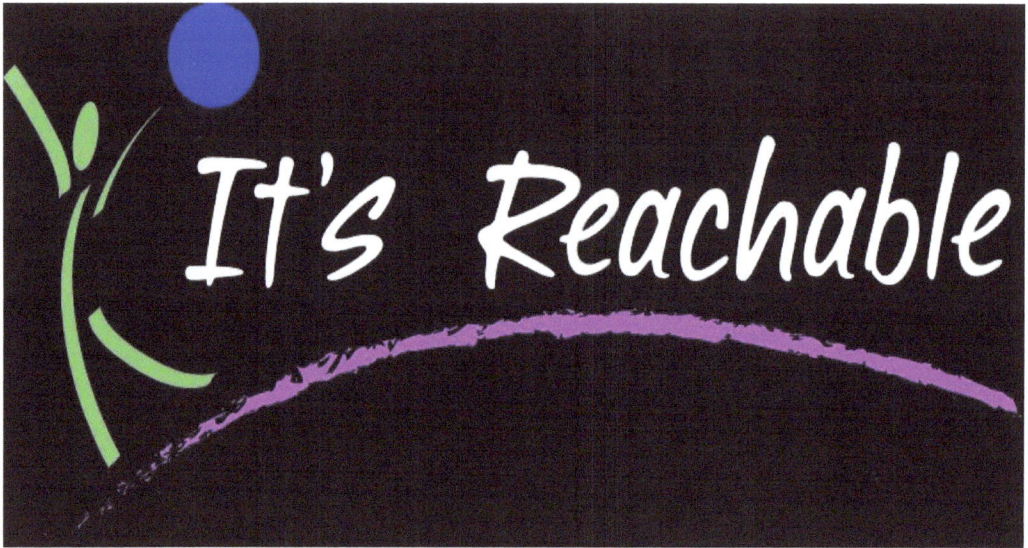

www.ingramcontent.com/pod-product-compliance
Lightning Source LLC
Chambersburg PA
CBHW041548040426
42447CB00002B/93

* 9 7 8 0 6 1 5 4 6 9 5 0 8 *